The Colorado River

The Colorado River

Carol B. Rawlins

SCHOLASTIC INC.

New York Toronto London Auckland Sydney
Mexico City New Delhi Hong Kong Buenos Aires

To my favorite water-person, Wendell G. Rawlins, my husband and good companion on the river journeys

NOTE TO READERS: Definitions for words in boldface can be found in the Glossary at the back of this book.

Copyright © 1999 by Franklin Watts, a division of Grolier Publishing Co., Inc. All rights reserved. Published by Scholastic Inc., 555 Broadway, New York, NY 10012. Printed in the U.S.A.

ISBN 0-531-18647-4

Contents

These streams in Rocky Mountain National Park, Colorado, are the source, or headwaters, of the Colorado River.

Chapter One

A Resource for Millions

High in the Rocky Mountains, gurgling water rushes under a footbridge. Near the beginning of its long trip downstream to the Gulf of California, the clear mountain stream picks up a load of muddy silt—loose, fine particles of soil that settle at the bottom of a river or lake—and becomes a fully grown, brick-red river. John Wesley Powell, an early river explorer, described the Colorado River as "too thick to drink, too thin to plow."

John Wesley Powell

John Wesley Powell (1834–1902) was born in Mount Morris, New York, and pioneered the exploration of the Colorado River.

The Colorado flows through these fields in southeastern California, one of many areas that are irrigated by the river.

Farther downstream, the river changes color again, from red to green. Its muddy load is filtered by some of the more than thirty dams through which the river passes on its way to the sea.

The Colorado River provides water to twenty million thirsty people in the U.S. Southwest and to fields growing green in the naturally arid, or dry, region. Cities, cattle, and crops far beyond the Colorado River Basin, the area drained by the river and its **tributaries,** depend on the Colorado for water.

Water is precious in the largest desert region on the North American continent, so claims on the river are great. Water authorities, politicians, American Indians, ranchers, farmers, cities, river-runners, environmentalists, seven states, and two nations haggle over water rights. The Colorado has been described as "the most litigated, regulated, and argued-about" river in the world.

A view of the Never Summer Mountains, which are part of the Rocky Mountains, in north central Colorado

Only one point is clear: the Colorado River system can't meet everyone's demands. In 1968, the National Academy of Sciences warned: "The Colorado River basin is closer than most other basins in the United States to utilizing the last drop of available water for man's needs."

The Colorado River originates in mountain streams fed by glaciers, large bodies of slowly moving ice. Its headwaters lie 14,000 feet (4,270 meters) above sea level in the Never Summer Mountains, which are part of the Rocky Mountains, in north central Colorado. It flows 1,450 miles (2,330 kilometers) west from the Continental Divide, then turns south, ending in the Gulf of California off the coast of Mexico.

The Continental Divide

Each continent has its own divide. In the United States, the Continental Divide runs north and south for 3,000 miles (4,830 km) along the highest elevations between Mexico and

National Academy of Sciences (NAS)

Founded in 1741, the NAS is dedicated to the study of science and engineering, and the pursuit of solutions to scientific problems.

Opposite: The route of the Colorado River through the south-western United States

Canada. Rivers that originate east of the Continental Divide flow east and become part of the Mississippi River system. The Mississippi River flows into the Gulf of Mexico, which then meets the Atlantic Ocean.

Rivers that originate west of the Divide flow west and empty into the Colorado River system. The Colorado River system includes the Colorado River and its tributaries—the Green, Gunnison, Dolores, San Juan, Virgin, Little Colorado, and Gila rivers. The Colorado River carries water from its tributaries to the Gulf of California (also called the Sea of Cortes) in Mexico and out to the Pacific Ocean. Before it reaches sea level, the Colorado drops nearly 3 miles (5 km).

Early explorers hoped the Colorado would carry freight and people throughout the Southwest, but the river disappointed them. In late spring, the turbulent "river of too much or too little," carrying logs and branches, huge boulders, and other kinds of debris, overflowed its banks. However, in late summer, the water became too shallow for continuous travel.

In 1935, Hoover Dam became the first of a series of modern dams built to bring the Colorado's seasonal floods under

A New Name

At one time, the Colorado River began with the confluence, or place where two rivers or streams meet, of the Green and the Grand rivers of Colorado. In 1921, the Colorado state legislature per-suaded the U.S. Congress to change the name of the Grand River to the Colorado River. The Grand River arm of the Colorado now appears on some maps as the Upper Colorado River.

10

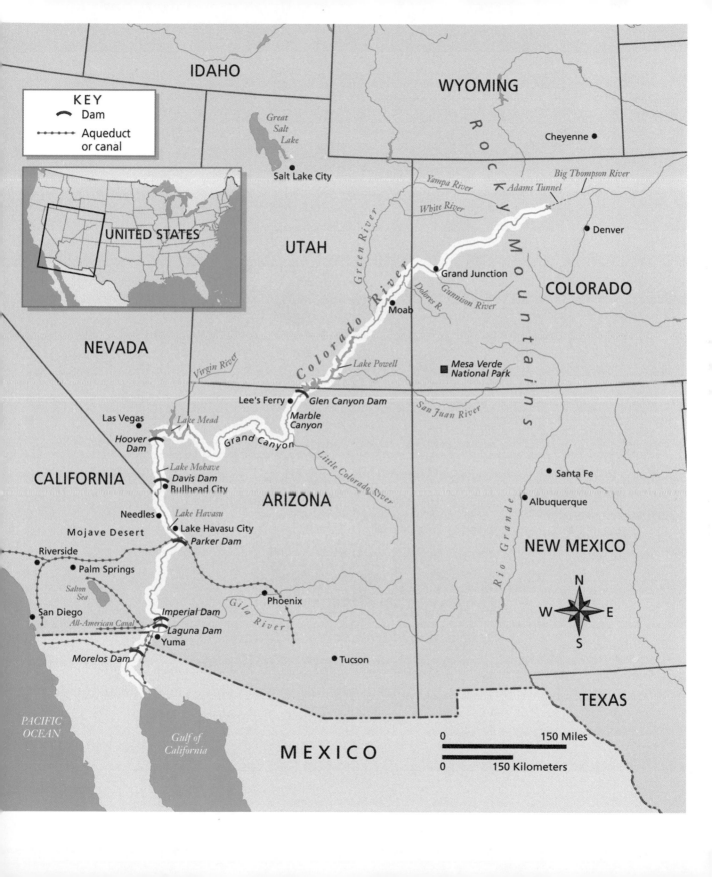

Hoover Dam was built not only to control the river's flooding, but to generate hydroelectric power for the surrounding area.

control. More than thirty dams and thousands of miles of irrigation canals, ditches, and pipes divert water from the system before the river reaches the gulf. Normally, the channel is dry from a few miles below the United States-Mexico border to the river delta.

Colorado River Delta

A river **delta** forms when **sediment** builds up near the **mouth** of a river. Fast-flowing, steep rivers carry more silt than slower rivers. A river deposits the extra material at its mouth when it slows to meet a larger body of water.

Each rainy season, the rapidly moving Colorado carried sediment downriver, building up the fan-shaped delta. The delta, sandbars in the river, and beaches in the Grand Canyon testify to the Colorado's land-building capacity. Today, the dams trap the river's land-building materials. The Colorado contributes little new material to the delta.

Photographs of the Colorado River delta taken from the air show a little water running across the delta into the Gulf of California. That water may be runoff from **tidal bores,** which are also called tidal surges. Tidal bores are huge waves caused by a rising tide that crash far up into a riverbed. Tidal bores on the Colorado River are second in size only to those on the Qiantang River in China. The Qiantang bores reach heights of 30 feet (9m).

The Colorado River Delta as seen from a height of 14,000 feet (4,267 m)

The Rocky Mountains are the highest point of the Colorado River Basin.

Chapter Two

The Colorado River Basin

The Colorado River drains 242,000 square miles (632,000 square km) in the United States, about one-twelfth of the continental land mass of the United States, and another 2,000 square miles (5,178 sq km) in Mexico. Parts of seven U.S. states lie in the Colorado River Basin: Colorado, Wyoming, Utah, New Mexico, Nevada, Arizona, and California.

Heavy snow and rainfall fill the upper end of the Colorado and its upper tributaries each year. The basin includes a variety of landforms: the western front of the Rocky Mountains, which are among the highest mountains in the United States, some smaller mountain ranges, fertile river valleys, canyons and other unusual rocky formations, arid land made usable by irrigation, and the largest desert in North America.

Carver of Canyons

The Colorado River Basin is a region of awesome natural beauty. American Indians have legends of the origin of this part of the world. Geologists, scientists who study the earth's layers of soil and rock, base their explanations for the spectacular Southwest on evidence revealed in the layers of rocks in the walls of the Grand Canyon.

The Grand Canyon was carved out of the Colorado Plateau, a 130,000-square-mile (337,000-sq-km) irregular land mass in the Four Corners region, where Colorado, New Mexico, Arizona, and Utah meet. Horizontal layers of sedimentary rock, formed from materials that settled out of ancient seas, characterize the plateau.

About sixty-five million years ago, a series of upheavals caused by forces deep within the earth lifted the land several

Grand Canyon National Park

The United States has protected areas of natural beauty, cultural importance, and recreational interest since 1872. Yellowstone Park was the first in a system of national parks, monuments, and recreation areas. In 1919, the Grand Canyon and a 1,904-square-mile (4,932-sq-km) area surrounding it became Grand Canyon National Park.

The Grand Canyon is one of the world's most famous examples of sedimentary rock.

miles. Five million years ago, new rumblings from far beneath the plateau produced another, smaller plateau.

For millions of years, the vigorous Colorado River flowed freely across the Colorado Plateau. The river carried silt along its journey from the mountains. Churning and grinding, the river split the plateau into two land masses. Over time, the river widened the split and carved out the magnificent Grand

Layered Rock

Sedimentary rock is usually easy to spot. It is made up of many layers of material, which are often different colors.

Today, the Colorado River continues to flow through, and carve, the Grand Canyon.

Canyon and the eighteen other deep-sided canyons that distinguish the Colorado Plateau.

By studying the walls of the Grand Canyon on each side of the Colorado River, geologists discovered that the two sides of

the plateau had once been connected. Though separated by the vast empty space of the huge canyon, the distinctive layers on each side match perfectly.

Water in Motion

Visitors to the Grand Canyon sometimes have a hard time believing that a river could carve a mile-deep hole. However, water in motion is one of nature's most powerful methods of altering a landscape.

Gravity pulls free-flowing water downhill toward sea level. As a trickle of water flows over the ground, it breaks off tiny bits of dirt, rock, and sand. In a process geologists call **transport,** the water carries that debris, which cuts into the surface of the earth's crust. The power of water to wear away, or erode, the land varies with the slope of the streambed. The Colorado River originates high in the mountains, descends very steeply in some places, and carries a heavy load of silt. These conditions made the river an amazingly effective sculptor of canyons.

Slow But Steady

The Colorado River began carving the Grand Canyon about six million years ago.

Generators within Hoover Dam create the hydroelectric power produced by the dam.

Chapter Three

Claiming The Colorado

The seven states in the Colorado River Basin signed the Colorado River Compact in 1922. Under the terms of the agreement, the Upper Basin states—Utah, Wyoming, Colorado, and New Mexico—receive and share 7.5 million **acre-feet** of river water each year. The Lower Basin states—California, Nevada, and Arizona—split an equal amount.

Terms of the Compact

An acre is larger than one-half of a football field. An acre-foot is the amount of

Water Rights

Water law in the western United States says that the first person to put a measurable quantity of water to beneficial use owns the rights to that water until he or she sells those rights to someone else. The rule is called "first in time, first in right." In the eastern United States, **riparian,** or river, rights belong to the person whose land is closest to the water.

water that is needed to cover 1 acre (0.4 hectare) of land to a depth of 12 inches (30 centimeters). One acre-foot equals about 325,000 gallons (1,231,750 liters). On average, an acre-foot of water meets the water needs of a family of four for one year.

In 1944, an international treaty guaranteed an additional 1.5 million acre-feet of river water to Mexico each year. However, the Colorado loses so much water before it reaches Mexico that only a trickle makes it to the Gulf of California.

To complicate the problem of who gets how much water, the estimate of the amount of water in the river each year was wrong. Evaporation of water into the air during **drought** years also reduced the amount of available water.

More than twenty years ago, the U.S. Bureau of Reclamation, which manages the dams and oversees the distribution of river water, warned that the average annual water supply from the Colorado River was inadequate to meet Compact and treaty agreements. Experts expect competition for water to become increasingly severe for all users by the year 2000, with many demands remaining unmet.

The Dams

More than thirty dams on the Colorado River make up part of the system that guarantees delivery of water to Compact members. The dams capture the heavy flow from rain and melting snow in the mountains in early summer. Water stored in the reservoirs behind the dams can be used when the amount of water in the river is low.

Ten of the dams release a controlled flow through turbines and generators to create **hydroelectric power.** The federal hydroelectric plants on the Colorado River produce almost 12 billion kilowatt-hours of energy each year.

The reservoirs behind some of the dams have become national recreation areas. Nearly thirty million fishermen, boaters, and water skiers visit the fifty-seven reservoirs and lakes on the Colorado River every year.

A view of the hydro-electric power plant at Glen Canyon Dam, in northern Arizona

Impressive Statistics

One of the highest concrete dams in the world, Hoover Dam is 726 feet (221 m) high and 1,244 feet (379 m) long. Elevators descend more than forty-four stories to reach its base. The dam contains enough concrete to pave a two-lane highway from New York City to San Francisco, California!

Lake Mead

Lake Mead is one of the world's largest man-made bodies of water.

Hoover Dam

Hoover Dam, the largest and best known of the dams on the Colorado River, is in Black Canyon, about 30 miles (48 km) southeast of Las Vegas, Nevada. Completed in 1936 and hailed as one of the world's engineering marvels, Hoover Dam made people think, for the first time, that the power of nature could be harnessed for their benefit.

Hoover Dam protects the Imperial Valley and other agricultural lands along the river from spring floods and seasonal droughts. Water stored in Lake Mead behind Hoover Dam irrigates more than 1 million acres (400,000 hectares) of land in Arizona, California, and Mexico. The lake is the nation's largest artificial reservoir. It can store 28.5 million acre-feet (about 9 trillion gallons, or 34 trillion liters) of water. In all, the Colorado River system irrigates 3.5 million acres (1.4 million hectares).

Hoover Dam focused the nation's attention on the Southwest. Plenty of water and a seemingly unlimited supply of electrical power transformed Las Vegas from a small desert town to one of the fastest-growing cities in the United States.

Glen Canyon Dam

Glen Canyon Dam is the most controversial of the dams on the Colorado. Upriver from the Grand Canyon and outside its eastern border, Glen Canyon Dam opened in 1964. Like Hoover Dam, Glen Canyon Dam was built to guarantee

*Glen Canyon Dam
and Lake Powell*

What's in a Name?

Lake Powell is named in honor of Major John Wesley Powell, who explored and named Glen Canyon.

delivery of water from the Upper Compact States to the Lower Compact States, provide flood control, store water, create recreation facilities, and produce hydroelectric power. The dam also was expected to extend the life of Hoover Dam by catching the silt carried by the Colorado River before it reached, and further damaged, the turbines of the dam.

The water trapped behind Glen Canyon Dam backs up into Glen Canyon. The flooded canyon forms part of the Lake Powell reservoir. Lake Powell has 1,960 miles (3,154 km) of shoreline and covers 250 square miles (648 sq km).

Glen Canyon Dam changed the Colorado River and the Grand Canyon in unexpected ways. One change was in the temperature of the water. When the Colorado flowed naturally, the sun warmed its water. In contrast, the water released through Glen Canyon Dam comes from the cold depths of Lake Powell. Some native varieties of fish that depend on seasonal warming of the river are now extinct. However, other varieties that flourish in cold water, such as trout, have been successfully introduced into the Colorado River.

When Glen Canyon Dam first opened, water from Lake Powell was released in periodic surges throughout the day all year round, as power needs rose and fell. One environmentalist compared the periodic surges to bulldozers plowing through the Grand Canyon several times each day. Wildlife suffered, islands washed away, and prehistoric Indian ruins along the river eroded. Today, engineers release water through the dam in moderate flows.

In a 1996 experiment to find out how the pre-dam Colorado River had done its land-building work, engineers allowed the Colorado River to flood a section of the Grand Canyon. They studied ways to regulate the river more naturally so it could rebuild islands and riverbanks within the canyon.

Boaters recreate on Lake Powell, which formed behind Glen Canyon Dam.

In this photograph, taken about 1940, a worker pauses beside one of the many machines used to construct the Adams Tunnel through the Rocky Mountains.

Chapter Four

Ditches and Diversions

The Colorado River system contributes more water to areas outside its basin than any other river system in the world. Some of the claims on the river are very old. A variety of ditches, tunnels, irrigation pipes, and canals deliver the promised water throughout the Colorado Basin and beyond.

The Grand Ditch

Since 1892, the Grand River Ditch has carried water from the Grand River (now the Upper Colorado) over the Continental Divide to the eastern front of the mountains outside the Colorado River Basin.

The Grand Ditch is a wooden **flume** almost 17 miles (27 km) long. The original leaky wooden flume is gradually being replaced by metal pipes, but much water has been wasted in the last one hundred years.

A Tunnel Through the Mountains

At Grand Lake, just outside Colorado's Rocky Mountain National Park, the 13-mile (21-km)-long Alva B. Adams tunnel cuts through the mountains to the Big Thompson River on the far (eastern) side of the mountains. The tunnel, completed in 1947 as part of the Colorado-Big Thompson River Project, delivers Colorado River water to cities such as

A cutaway view of the Adams Tunnel shows the tunnel's route through the mountains.

COLORADO–BIG THOMPSON PROJECT
CONTINENTAL DIVIDE
WESTERN SLOPE   EASTERN SLOPE

ALVA B. ADAMS TUNNEL

COLORADO RIVER   BIG THOMPSON RIVER

Denver, Colorado, and to 720,000 acres (291,000 hectares) of farmland on the eastern front of the mountains.

Diversions on the San Juan River

Diversions, such as **aqueducts** and **irrigation canals,** are artificial means of channeling water to another location. Diversions on the San Juan River, one of the Colorado's major tributaries, are a good example of the way decisions made in one part of the river affect the entire system.

The San Juan River rises in the San Juan Mountains of southwestern Colorado, which receive as much as 50 inches (127 centimeters) of rain a year. Since 1938, three irrigation ditches have diverted San Juan River water away from the Colorado, sending the water to the much drier Río Grande Basin.

In the 1970s, hydrologists, scientists who study the activity of water, tried to increase rainfall in the San Juan Mountains by seeding clouds over the mountains. Increasing normal precipitation by cloud-seeding might be possible, but the long-term effects on the **environment** are unknown. More experiments are planned.

Rainmaking

Seeding involves sprinkling clouds with dry ice or chemicals in an effort to cause rainfall.

Aqueducts

Several of the nation's most impressive aqueducts begin at Parker Dam, 150 miles (241 km) below Hoover Dam at Lake Havasu, Arizona. The Central Arizona Project carries Colorado River water 335 miles (539 km) east to Phoenix and

Part of the aqueduct system of the Central Arizona Project, which carries Colorado River water from Lake Havasu, Arizona, to Phoenix and Tucson

Tucson. The 242-mile (390-km)-long Colorado River Aqueduct and the 71-mile (114-km)-long San Diego Aqueduct carry water to cities in southern California.

Irrigation Canals

At Yuma, Arizona, the last U.S. city on the Colorado's route, two major canals divert water from the river. The Coachella Canal flows north toward Riverside, California. The All-American Canal flows west irrigating the Imperial Valley, one of the country's major food-producing regions. Without Colorado River water, nothing would grow in Imperial Valley.

A Diversion in Mexico

At Morelos Dam, south of Yuma, where the Colorado crosses into Mexico, the river is diverted again. An irrigation canal carries the water underground to nearby crops. The river channel is empty, except in times of unusually heavy rain, until it meets the Hardy River and continues to the Gulf of California.

The fate of the Salton Sea continues to concern both scientists and environmentalists.

The Salton Sea

The Salton Sea, south of Indio, California, developed when the Colorado River flooded the low Salton Basin between 1904 and 1907. The Salton Sea is 232 feet (71 m) below sea level and has no outlet to the ocean. Runoff water from irrigation canals drains into the Salton Sea. Originally filled with freshwater from the Colorado River, the Salton Sea is now nearly 30 percent saltier than the ocean. The salinity, or saltiness of the water, is expected to increase. Urban planners hope to channel fresh irrigation runoff for their own use before the water runs into the Salton Sea. If that happens, the Salton Sea will become even saltier. Some scientists believe no fish and wildlife will survive. The Salton Sea could become a dead sea.

Chapter Five

People of the Colorado Basin

At one time, grass covered much of the Colorado River Basin. Rainfall and streams were ample. Herds of animals, including **mammoths,** provided food and skins for clothing and shelter for the people who inhabited the basin 15,000 years ago.

By 10,000 B.C., the glaciers of the Pleistocene Ice Age had begun to retreat.

The climate grew hotter and drier. Herds of animals became scarce and the people disappeared.

We know that people had returned again to the Colorado River Basin by 2145 B.C. That is the date given to a split-twig animal figure found in a cave at the Grand Canyon. The figure is the earliest Indian **artifact** found in the region.

The Hohokam people on the north bank of the Gila River, one of the Colorado's tributaries, may have constructed the first irrigation ditches in the system. They watered their crops from ditches linked to a 3-mile (4.8-km)-long canal from the Gila River.

Split-twig animal figures such as this one can now be seen in the museum at Grand Canyon National Park.

The Ancient Ones

The Anasazi, whose name means "ancient ones," are the best known of the early people of the Colorado Plateau. They lived in the Four Corners region.

At first, the Anasazi gathered plants and hunted small game for food. However, by the first century A.D., they grew corn, squash, and beans in the rich soil the Colorado River

Opposite: These ancient pictures of a man and hands were drawn by Anasazi Indians on canyon walls in Utah thousands of years ago.

Priceless Trash

Archeologists, historians of the ancient past, have learned much about the Anasazi from their trash heaps and storage areas. The dry climate preserved many artifacts, including baskets and pottery. The Anasazi discarded their trash in pits called middens and stored their grain in high small **granaries** in the upper reaches of the canyons, safe from animals and the weather.

Were the Anasazi Cannibals?

Another theory introduced in late 1998 to explain the disappearance of the Ancient Ones speculates that the Anasazi practiced **cannibalism** and died out as a result of it. The theory is based on archeological findings, and many experts have accepted the explanation.

deposited on the canyon floors. The Anasazi moved to the rims of the canyons, where firewood was plentiful, during the cold winter months.

During various times, the Anasazi lived in caves, pit houses (dugouts with wooden walls and roofs), pueblos, which were towns of several-storied apartment houses, and cliff dwellings.

By the 1300s, the Anasazi disappeared from the plateau. The reasons are not fully known, but hundreds of square miles of land had been **deforested** for firewood and roof beams. A series of droughts in the Southwest, lasting more than one hundred years, further deforested the land. As the population grew, nutrients in the soil were used up. The Anasazi may have moved away in small groups over a period of time.

Visitors explore ancient Anasazi cliff dwellings found in Mesa Verde National Park, Colorado.

The Spanish

By the 16th century, Spain was exploring the "New World" of the Americas that Christopher Columbus first saw in 1492. In Mexico and Central and South America, the Spaniards found gold and silver. Searching for more treasure, the Spanish moved north into present-day California and the Colorado River Basin.

In 1540, Hernando Cortés, the leader of the Spanish **conquistadors,** sent Francisco Vásquez de Coronado and his men to search for Cibola, seven mythical golden cities. After a skirmish with the local Indians, the Spaniards claimed the territory for Spain. Spanish metal helmets and swords still turn up in the deserts of New Mexico and Arizona.

Sent by Coronado to confirm Hopi Indian stories of a "great river flowing in a chasm with walls colored like gold," Captain García López de Cárdenas and a small band of Spanish soldiers were the first Europeans to record seeing the Colorado River and the Grand Canyon.

In 1540, the Cárdenas party arrived on the south rim of the Grand Canyon. Cárdenas sent three men to find passage across the river at the bottom of the canyon. The men reported the great depth of the canyon, but could not find a safe way across the wider-than-expected river. Cárdenas concluded that the canyon was "worthless" to Spain. More than two hundred years passed before another European recorded a visit to the canyon.

Hernando Cortés (1485–1547) is one of the best-known Spanish conquistadors.

Father Garcés (second from right) encountered the Havasupai Indians of the Grand Canyon in 1776.

Meanwhile, Spanish ships sailed into the Gulf of California looking for a water route to the interior. In 1540, Hernando de Alarcón was the first European to sail up the Colorado River.

In 1776, Father Francisco Tomas Garcés, from a **mission** near Tucson, Arizona, climbed down into one of the side canyons of the Grand Canyon and found a small tribe of Indians living there—the Havasupai. Garcés was the first man to consistently refer to the Colorado as the "Río Colorado," the Red-Colored River.

In 1821, Spain surrendered control of the region to Mexico. Twenty-five years later, the United States and Mexico went to war over boundaries and ownership of land. When the war ended in 1848, the United States gained the territories of New Mexico, Arizona, Texas, and California.

The Americans

From 1820 to 1840, trappers and traders from Europe and the United States, who became known as "mountain men," crossed the Rocky Mountains and followed the Colorado River in search of beaver pelts. Well-dressed gentlemen in the

United States and Europe wore tall hats made of beaver fur. The beavers were hunted almost to extinction before beaver hats went out of style.

Members of the Church of Jesus Christ of Latter-day Saints, called Mormons, settled the region north of the Grand Canyon in the mid-1800s. The Mormons and the federal government argued about who controlled the land the Mormons settled. The Mormons also had conflicts with American Indians in the region over water, game, and free movement over land the Indians considered theirs.

Trappers watering their horses in the Colorado River were a common sight during the mid-1800s.

Camels Run Wild

Lieutenant Edward Fitzgerald Beale of the U.S. Army surveyed the region south of the Grand Canyon. Beale persuaded Jefferson Davis, the U.S. Secretary of War (who would later head the Confederacy), to purchase eighty camels for carrying mail, hauling freight, and exploring the desert. Soon all but one of the Arab camel drivers quit, overwhelmed by the canyons, the Indians, and the desert. American mule drivers never did get the knack of keeping loads on the camels' backs, and the noisy camels stampeded the horses.

When the Civil War began in 1861, the camels were set loose. They roamed the Southwest for years, wandering into towns and startling people and livestock. Eventually, all the camels became food for hunters when wildlife was scarce.

Joseph C. Ives

Tension between the Mormons and the federal government caused President James Buchanan to send army troops to Utah in 1857. The government needed a southern route to supply federal troops in Utah and other posts in the West, so Lieutenant Joseph Christmas Ives was sent to see how far up the Colorado River steamships could travel.

Ives shipped pieces of a steamboat to the mouth of the Colorado River, where it was reassembled. The Ives party traveled 350 miles (563 km) up the river from Fort Yuma, in the Arizona Territory, to Black Canyon, 78 miles (126 km) from the Grand Canyon. On the trip, Ives's men spotted Beale's camels. In Black Canyon, the boat broke up on the rocks, so the party traveled overland to the Grand Canyon.

Ives's expedition did little to create interest in the Colorado River as a cross-country route. As earlier explorers had, Ives concluded: "The region is, of course, altogether valueless. It can be approached only from the south, and after entering it there is nothing to do but leave. Ours has been the first, and will doubtless be the last, party of whites to visit this profitless locality. It seems intended by nature that the Colorado River, along the greater portion of its lonely and majestic way, shall be forever unvisited and undisturbed."

John Wesley Powell

After the Civil War ended in 1865, the "Arid Region," the name given to the unmapped area between the Great Plains and California, aroused considerable interest. In 1869, Major John Wesley Powell, a one-armed retired Union officer, college teacher, and amateur naturalist, led the first documented trip down the Green and Colorado rivers. Ten men in four boats explored Cataract Canyon, Glen Canyon, and 277 miles (446 km) inside the Grand Canyon.

In this photograph, taken about 1875, John Wesley Powell (right) is pictured with Paiute Chief Tau-Gu.

As the party entered the Grand Canyon, Powell wrote: "With some feeling of anxiety we enter a new canyon this morning. We have learned to observe closely the texture of the rock. In softer strata we have quiet river; in harder we find **rapids** and falls. Below us are limestones and hard sandstones which we found in Cataract Canyon. This bodes toil and danger."

Powell was correct. The boats could not navigate the rapids. Many of the boats had to be portaged, or carried overland past rough water. Powell's official report, *The Exploration of the Colorado River of the West and Its Tributaries*, and his newspaper stories informed and excited the public. In l871–72, Powell conducted a second river expedition. His work as an explorer-scientist opened the West. He literally put the Grand Canyon and the Colorado River on the map.

Many people find a white water rafting trip down the Colorado River an exhilarating adventure.

Chapter Six

A Trip Down the River

Small glacier-fed streams cascade down the snow-capped Never Summer Mountains west of the Continental Divide to form the Colorado River. The river meanders slowly across beautiful valley meadows surrounded by tall, dark forests that climb up the valley walls to higher elevations. The Grand Ditch, the flume that carries river water over the Continental Divide, can be seen about halfway up the mountains.

A moose feeds on the plant life in the cool waters of the Colorado River.

Leaving the mountains, the Colorado flows through the green meadows of river valleys. Bogs and marshes along the river form natural storage areas to hold water in the summer. Trumpeter swans, sandbill cranes, and other birds shelter their young in the tall grass. Moose feed on water plants. Beavers build dams along quiet tributaries, creating ponds for nesting wildlife.

Cutthroat trout struggle to jump rapids on their annual return upstream to spawn in the high mountain streams where they were born. Bald eagles, living in trees along the banks of the river, feed on the trout. Migrating birds follow the river.

The river swells as mountain creeks and small rivers join it. The town of Grand Junction, Colorado, lies at the confluence of the Colorado and the Gunnison rivers. Peaches, pears, and a variety of other crops grow in the broad, fertile Grand River Valley.

Between Grand Junction and Moab, Utah, the Colorado crosses the Colorado-Utah border and picks up water from the Dolores River. In northeastern Utah, the Yampa and White rivers flow into Wyoming's Green River, making it the most powerful arm of the Colorado River. The Green River joins the Colorado south of Moab, Utah. The combined waters flow into Glen Canyon National Recreation Area.

Below the junction, the land becomes dusty and dry. Sagebrush offers wildlife little shelter from the heat. Pronghorn deer and whitetail jack rabbits must find moisture in the vegetation. Herds of wild **mustangs** drink from the river.

Swirling currents, blowing sand from river sandbars, and a sign warn people of what's ahead in Cataract Canyon. "DANGER. Cataract Canyon. Hazardous Rapids—2 miles. Permit required." The 18 1/2 miles (30 km) of continuous rapids in Cataract Canyon provide good practice for the 277 miles (446 km) of **white water** coming up in the Grand Canyon.

The river flows on into Lake Powell, the heart of Glen Canyon National Recreation Area. The San Juan River, another tributary, joins the Colorado in Lake Powell.

The Colorado crosses the Utah-Arizona border at Glen Canyon Dam. As it enters Lake Powell, the river is warm, brick-red, and filled with silt. Leaving Glen Canyon Dam, the

Wild mustangs, long a symbol of the American West, find much-needed water in the Colorado River.

Navajo brothers in Arizona herd their family's sheep and goats near the river.

water is cold, blue-green, and clear, its silt settled to the bottom of Lake Powell.

Navajo and Hopi Indians graze sheep on the left bank of the river. Ahead, at Page, Arizona, yellow-gray smoke rises from the Navajo Generating Station, which provides electric power for the Navajo and Hopi Indian reservations.

At the settlement of Lee's Ferry, the reddish-brown Paria River meets the now-green Colorado. The two colors flow side by side, eventually mixing.

Lee's Ferry

John Doyle Lee established ferry service across the Colorado River in 1871, using a boat discarded by John Wesley Powell. At one time, Lee's Ferry, in Arizona Territory, was the only place where people could cross the Colorado River until Grand Wash Cliffs, 277 miles (446 km) ahead. Lee, a Mormon, was arrested in 1874 for allegedly leading a massacre of non-Mormons twenty years earlier. He was executed in 1877. Emma Lee, the seventeenth of Lee's nineteen wives, operated the ferry until 1879. Other owners continued service until 1928, when three men drowned and the ferry shut down. In 1929, Navajo Bridge, built over the river in Marble Canyon, opened. Navajo Bridge is the only place automobiles can cross the river until Hoover Dam—300 miles (483 km) away.

The Colorado River Corridor

Scientists refer to the 277 miles (446 km) between Lee's Ferry and Grand Wash Cliffs at the far end of the Grand Canyon as the Colorado River Corridor. The Little Colorado River joins the Colorado from the Painted Desert to the southeast. The replenished Colorado is 300 feet (90 m) wide, with a swift, strong current, as it enters the Grand Canyon.

Rapids Ahead!

Some of the Grand Canyon's rapids are among the most dangerous in the world. Experienced river guides pilot large rubber rafts or **dories** filled with adventurers through the canyon. Good river guides know the river well. They keep track of changes in river currents and water levels, both of which change when water is released upriver through Glen Canyon Dam.

Riparian Life

The community of living things in and along the banks of a river is called a riparian community. Cottonwoods, horsetails, and several varieties of willows grow by the river, but tamarix, a non-native tree, is the most common plant. Introduced in the early 1800s, tamarix forces out native plants. Its deep roots consume available water before it can reach more shallow-rooted plants.

Mammals near the river include ringtail cats, which have been said to befriend prospectors, spotted skunks, river otters,

A Geologist's Dream

The walls of the Grand Canyon provide a perfect classroom for geologists and others interested in a clear record of Earth's development. The 6,600 feet (2,012 m) between the top and the bottom of the canyon record two billion years of geological history. Each colorful stratum, or layer, in the canyon walls gives clues to the environment in which that particular stratum formed.

Bighorn sheep are a species of wild sheep found only in North America.

A visitor along the rapids at Lava Falls

beavers, and several varieties of mice. Mule deer and **endangered** bighorn sheep inhabit cliffs along some sections of the river. River reptiles include lizards and the unique pink-colored Grand Canyon rattlesnake.

Because the yearly floods are controlled, new growth creates places for birds not formerly common in the area. Endangered peregrine falcons, for example, are increasing in numbers.

The Colorado flows on past Havasu Canyon, Arizona, one of the most beautiful of the side canyons. Vulvan's Anvil, where volcanoes once erupted, warns that Lava Falls Rapid, a 34-foot (10-m) waterfall, is ahead.

Below the Grand Canyon

The canyon walls give way to open desert, and the river crosses the Arizona-Nevada border. Huge Lake Mead lies ahead. The river is slow and clear as it leaves Hoover Dam and flows between the dark, steep, rocky walls of Black Canyon, where Ives smashed his steamboat in 1858. Nearby, Boulder City provided housing and services for the workers who built Hoover Dam. Ahead, 500 miles (805 km) of calm river and a string of reservoirs beckon.

The river moves on into Lake Mohave, above Davis Dam. Below the dam, the river flows under a bridge at Bullhead City, Arizona. On the other side of the bridge, the bright lights of Laughlin, Nevada, shine. Sightseeing boats and privately owned craft move up and down the river. On the Bullhead City side, many-storied houses line the riverbank. The lower stories were built to accommodate water when the Colorado flooded them each year.

Below the two towns, Colorado River water irrigates acres of green farmland, starting in the midst of the surrounding yellowish-brown Mojave Desert. The fertile river soil produces alfalfa, cotton, wheat, and sudan grass.

The river passes more farms. Levees, canals, and irrigation pumps channel river water into the fields. Wildlife is scarce here. The ground and irrigation runoff returning to the river are salty. Downriver, the salinity of the river will be a problem for agriculture, fish, and wildlife.

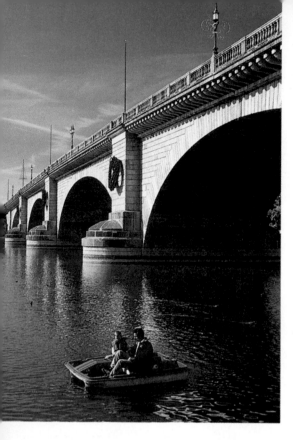

Boaters and tourists have enjoyed the London Bridge at Lake Havasu City, Arizona, since it was imported from England in 1971.

The Colorado reaches Needles, California, a railroad town and an oasis for travelers crossing the wide Mojave Desert. Meteorologists frequently cite Needles as the town with the hottest temperature in the nation.

Here, the river slows. Side creeks and the slow-moving river create a marshy wildlife reserve. Raccoons, coyotes, and mice keep small and large birds company. Small islands separate the river into channels. **Lagoons** have formed along the riverbanks. At Lake Havasu City, Arizona, tourists can see a portion of the London Bridge, imported from England by a real estate developer.

Several national wildlife reserves and lakes surround the river near Imperial Dam and Laguna Dam. The All-American Canal, one of the longest irrigation canals in the world, delivers Colorado River water from Imperial Dam to the fields of Coachella Valley and Imperial Valley.

The Gila River joins the Colorado at Yuma, Arizona. The Gila, the fourth major tributary of the Colorado River system, usually has a dry riverbed, except in times of heavy rain.

Below the Mexican Border

Near Yuma, the Colorado River crosses into Mexico and becomes the Río Colorado. The Río Colorado flows into Morelos Dam and comes out in an irrigation canal that carries the water to nearby farms. The riverbed is usually empty from here to the juncture with the Río Hardy.

Abandoned vacation homes and camps built in the river's free-flowing days stand along the riverbanks. A few herons and the barren salt flats are clues that water once flowed. West of the empty Río Colorado bed, the Río Hardy, also flowing south, collects unused irrigation water and returns it to the Colorado.

The little water remaining in the river flows into the huge delta at the mouth of the river. Most river travelers leave the river before this point. There is usually not enough water to float even a shallow river craft. At other times, tidal surges from the Gulf of California crash up into the almost-empty riverbed and overwhelm small boats.

The huge Gulf of California, once called the Sea of Cortes, is ahead on the far side of the delta. The Pacific Ocean is beyond the gulf. The Colorado River has completed its journey.

The Río Colorado in Baja California, Mexico, serves as a boundary between the United States and Mexico.

Glossary

acre-foot—the amount of water needed to cover 1 acre (0.4 hectare) of land to a depth of 12 inches (30 cm), about 325,000 gallons (1,231,750 liters)

aqueduct—a pipe or canal that carries water from one place to another

artifact—a handmade object, such as a tool, from a particular culture

cannibalism—the eating of the flesh of an animal by another animal of the same kind

conquistadors—the Spanish word for conquerors, leaders in the Spanish conquest of America

deforest—the process of clearing land of trees or forests

delta—triangular-shaped land at the mouth of a river that is formed by the buildup of sediment deposited by a river

dories—flat-bottomed boats with high, flaring sides

drought—a period of little rainfall

cndangered—in danger of becoming extinct

environment—the conditions that surround living communities: climate, soil, plants and animals, and quality of air and water

flume—an inclined channel for moving water

granaries—places used to store grain

hydroelectric power—electricity created by falling water turning the turbines in a generator, usually within a dam

irrigation canal—an artificial ditch created to supply water to land

lagoon—a shallow pool connected to a larger body of water

mammoths—extinct elephant-like mammals with long hair and tusks

mission—a church or other place where missionaries live and work

mouth—the place where a stream or river enters a larger body of water

mustangs—wild horses that are found mostly on the plains of the western United States

rapids—steep descent in a river where the water current is swift

riparian—related to a river or other body of water

sediment—matter that settles at the bottom of a liquid; material, such as rocks, sand, or dirt that has been carried to a place by water

tidal bores—huge waves from the incoming tide that crash into a river channel

transport—the process of transferring or carrying debris that cuts into the earth's surface

tributaries—streams or rivers that flow into a larger stream or river

white water—frothy water, such as rapids or waterfalls

To Find
Out More

Books (Non-Fiction)

Bledsoe, Sara. *Colorado*. Minneapolis, MN: Lerner, 1993.

Bruns, Roger A. *John Wesley Powell: Explorer of the Grand Canyon*. Springfield, NJ: Enslow, 1997.

Gaines, Ann. *John Wesley Powell and the Great Surveys of the American West*. New York: Chelsea House, 1992.

Heinrichs, Ann. *California*. Danbury, CT: Children's Press, 1998.

Radlauer, Ruth. *Grand Canyon National Park*. Chicago: Childrens Press, 1984.

Rawlins, Carol. *The Grand Canyon*. Chatham, NJ: Raintree Steck-Vaughn, 1995.

Books (Fiction)

George, Jean Craighead. *River Rats, Inc.* E.P. Dutton, 1979.

Henry, Marguerite. *Brighty of the Grand Canyon*. Aladdin Books, 1991.

Hobbs, Will. *Downriver.* Atheneum, 1991.

Video

Cadillac Desert. Colorado River segment, PBS, 1997.

CD-ROM

"Colorado River." Compton's Interactive Encyclopedia, 1994.

Organizations and Online Sites

Colorado River
http://www.fish-colorado-river.com
Take a guided tour down the Colorado River. Photos and links to related sites are included.

Glen Canyon Dam

http://www.nps.gov/glca/

Sponsored by the National Park Service, this site includes all the information you need to plan a visit to Glen Canyon Dam. You can even take a virtual tour of the dam and find links to many other sites.

Grand Canyon

http://www.grandcanyon.org

This site contains a bookstore, maps and information about Grand Canyon National Park, and links to related sites.

Hoover Dam

http://www.hooverdam.com.

Enter the virtual visitor center for a virtual tour of the inside and outside of Hoover Dam. Sponsored by the U.S. Department of the Interior–Bureau of Reclamation, this site also includes full-color photos and links to other sites.

U.S. Army Corps of Engineers
Regional Brochures
CEWES-IM-MV-N
3909 Halls Ferry Road
Vicksburg, MS 39180-6199

You can request brochures with information about lakeside recreation in the Southwest.

World-Wide Research and Publishing Company
P.O. Box 3073
Casper, WY 82602
For a small fee, you can obtain National Parkways publications about Grand Canyon National Park, Rocky Mountain National Park, or Mesa Verde National Park.

Periodicals

Arizona Highways and *National Geographic* magazines have many issues that contain articles about the Colorado River.

A Note On Sources

In San Diego County, where I live, water diverted from the Colorado River provides three-quarters of the water we drink and use for irrigation, so we San Diegans keep close tabs on the state of the river. Our newspapers keep us informed about what's new with the river and water agreements. My husband and I are what the *Los Angeles Times* calls "water people," which means we are fascinated with all the Earth's rivers. We like to follow rivers and see what we find along the way.

River, by Colin Fletcher, is the account of a trip down the Colorado. Another fascinating book by Colin Fletcher, *The Man who Walked Through Time*, is about Fletcher's hike through the Grand Canyon. *The Colorado River Through the Grand Canyon*, by Steven W. Carothers and Bryan T. Brown, and *Grand Canyon*, by Joseph Wood Krutch, are other excellent sources. You can check out John Wesley Powell's *The Exploration of the Colorado River of the West and Its Tributaries* from most public libraries. *Arizona Highways* magazine and *National Geographic* frequently feature the Colorado River.

Many public television stations throughout the country show *Cadillac Desert*, about the Colorado River.

For fictional accounts of the Colorado River, you might want to read *River Rats, Inc.*, by Jean Craighead George, and *Downriver*, by Will Hobbs. Marguerite Henry's *Brighty of the Grand Canyon* is about a mule that lives in the canyon.

—*Carol B. Rawlins*

Index

Numbers in *italics* indicate illustrations.

About the Author

Carol Blashfield Rawlins has deep midwestern roots. Born in Wisconsin, she attended public schools in Illinois, graduated from Ohio Wesleyan University, and then returned to Illinois to teach high school English, history, and social studies. Later she moved to Topeka, Kansas, where she raised a daughter and son, attended graduate school at the University of Kansas, and worked for the State of Kansas.

A Californian for more than a decade, Carol and her husband enjoy following rivers from beginning to end, documenting what they see along the way. Today, they live in Santee, near San Diego. Ms. Rawlins is also the author of *The Orinoco River* for FranklinWatts.